D1306954

Drawing MONSTERS Step-by-Step

Drawing VAMPIRES

Carter Hayn

WINDMILL
BOOKS ™

New York

Published in 2013 by Windmill Books, LLC

CREDITS
Book Design: Nathalie Beullens-Maoui
Art by Planman, Ltd.

Photo Credits: Cover, p. 18 Todd Keith/Vetta/Getty Images; p. 4 Christophe Testi/Shutterstock.com (pencil); p. 5 Obak/Shutterstock.com (paper), Paul Matthew Photography/Shutterstock.com (eraser), 2happy/Shutterstock.com (marker), Iv Nikolny/Shutterstock.com (pencils); p. 6 Tim Flach/Stone +/Getty Images; p. 8 Imagno/Hulton Archive/Getty Images; p. 10 Universal Pictures/Moviepix/Getty Images; p. 12 Silver Screen Collection/Moviepix/Getty Images; p. 14 © Globe Photos/ZUMA Press; p. 16 Silver Screen Collection/Archive Photos/Getty Images; p. 20 vectorbomb/Vetta/Getty Images.

Cataloging-in-Publication Data

Hayn, Carter.
Drawing Vampires / by Carter Hayn.
   p. cm. — (Drawing monsters step-by-step)
Includes index.
ISBN 978-1-61533-691-3 (library binding) — ISBN 978-1-61533-702-6 (pbk.) — ISBN 978-1-61533-703-3 (6-Pack)
1. Vampires in art — Juvenile literature. 2. Monsters in art — Juvenile literature. 3. Drawing — Technique — Juvenile literature. I. Title.
NC825.V36 H39 2013
743.8'7—dc23

Manufactured in the United States of America

For more great fiction and nonfiction, go to www.windmillbooks.com.

CPSIA Compliance Information: Batch #BW13WM: For further information contact Windmill Books, New York, New York at 1-866-478-0556.

Contents

Creatures of the Night

Vampires are **mythical** creatures that have existed in popular folklore since before ancient Roman times. Vampires are monsters that feed on human blood. They only come out at night.

The story *The Vampyre*, written in 1819, was the first to describe a vampire the way most people think of

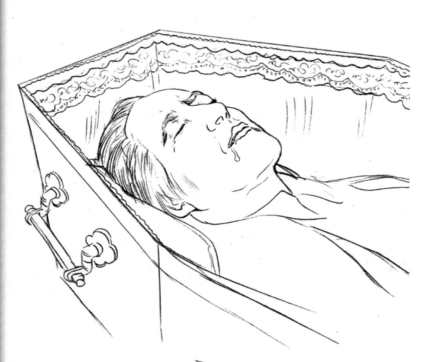

them today. These defining traits include **immortality**, ability to transform into a bat or a wolf, and sleeping in a coffin.

In this book, you will learn much more about these creepy monsters as you also learn how to draw them.

PENCIL

YOU WILL NEED THE FOLLOWING SUPPLIES:

ERASER

PAPER

RULER

COLORED PENCILS

MARKER

Real Vampires

There are many myths surrounding vampires. One story is that they turn into bats at night to search for **prey**. This **legend** might be based on the fact that there are some

species of bats that eat only other animals' blood. These bats are called vampire bats.

Vampire bats that live in South America, Central America, and Mexico. They feed on the blood of horses, cattle, and other livestock. They come out at night and use their sharp teeth to make a small cut in their prey's skin, from which they drink its blood. This is also how vampires are said to feed.

STEP 1
Draw two circles.

STEP 4
Draw the outline of
the wings and branch.
Draw the eyes, ears,
and snout.

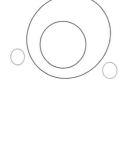

STEP 2
Draw small
ovals around
the body to
act as guides.

STEP 5
Add the hairs to
the body. Draw
the details on
the paws. Erase
the guide ovals.

STEP 3
Join the ovals with lines
to form the legs and the
beginning of the wings.

STEP 6
Add details and
color to your bat.

A Ruthless Count

One of the best known vampires is Count Dracula. Bram Stoker created this character in his 1897 novel, *Dracula*. Stoker based his character on a real-life, ruthless prince named Vlad III from what is present-day Romania. This prince was known as Vlad the Impaler, because he killed people by impaling them, or running them through with a stake.

The name "Dracula" means "the dragon." The prince's father took the name after he joined the Order of the Dragon. The Order of the Dragon was a group of knights that fought the Turks during the Crusades. Today, "Dracula" is no longer associated with dragons, but with the most famous vampire.

Vlad the Impaler had a reputation for cruelty. It is said that as many as 100,000 people were killed under his reign.

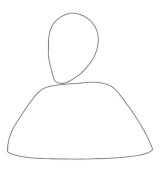

STEP 1
Draw the outline of the head. Add the shape for the body as shown.

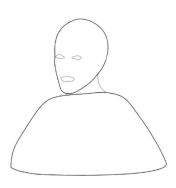

STEP 2
Draw the eyes and mouth. Add the outline of the neck.

STEP 3
Draw the outline of the headgear and the hair.

STEP 4
Draw the buttons on the shirt. Add details to the headgear.

STEP 5
Draw the eyebrows, mustache, and more facial details. Add details to the clothes and hair. Erase the guides.

STEP 6
Add details to the facial features. Draw the folds in the clothing. Color your drawing.

Bram Stocker's *Dracula* inspired two plays as well as many movies. In 1927, the actor Bela Lugosi played the title character in one of the plays. He was asked in 1931 to play the character in *Dracula*, the first horror movie with sound! Originally from Hungary, Lugosi used his own Eastern European accent to play the character.

Lugosi is considered by some to be the best Dracula. This is because he set the standard for future actors playing the part with his accent, his slow and mysterious voice, and the way he moved. Actors sometimes imitate Lugosi when playing Dracula.

Bela Lugosi tried not to blink while being filmed for the *Dracula*. He did this to seem even scarier.

STEP 1

Draw a round shape for the head and a boxy shape for the body.

STEP 2

Draw small circles and ovals around the body.

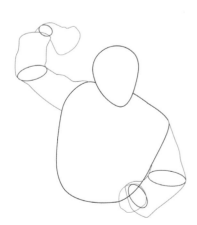

STEP 3

Use the circles and ovals to guide you in drawing the arms and hands.

STEP 4

Draw the outline of the hair. Add the cape's collar and the outline of the vest.

STEP 5

Draw the eyes, the eyebrows, the nose, and the mouth. Add details to the clothes. Draw the fingers. Erase the guide shapes.

STEP 6

Add more facial details. Add more details to the clothing. Color your drawing.

A Vampire Shows Fangs

Another famous Count Dracula is British actor Christopher Lee. Lee acted in five Dracula movies from 1958 to 1970. The first of these movies was *The Horror of Dracula*. In it, Christopher Lee wore fake fangs and also contact lenses to give Dracula scary eyes.

In the movie *Dracula: Prince of Darkness*, Christopher Lee had no lines! He would hiss at his victims.

The Horror of Dracula was the first Dracula movie in color. The blood was creepier than it had ever been before!

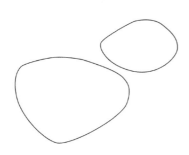

STEP 1
Begin your drawing with two round shapes.

STEP 4
Add the details to the inside and outside of the coffin. Add the hairline and the pleats of the cape.

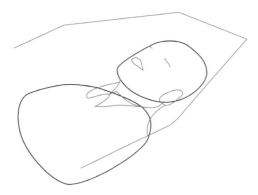

STEP 2
Draw lines to form the outline of coffin. Draw the collar of the cape, the eyes, the nose and the ear.

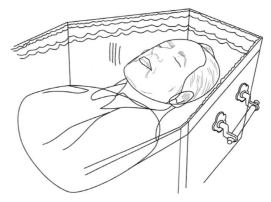

STEP 5
Draw the hair, eyebrows, nose, and blood from the mouth. Erase extra lines.

STEP 3
Draw more detail for the coffin. Draw the handle of the coffin.

STEP 6
Add details to the face, the coffin, and the clothes. Color your drawing.

From Books to Movies

In recent years, new **generations** of vampires have risen, both in movies and books. Anne Rice's Vampire Chronicles novels have been popular since the fist book, *Interview with the Vampire*, appeared in 1976. There have been two movies based on these novels. Stephenie Meyer's Twilight novels have also been very popular. They have been made into five movies, which have brought in more than $3 billion in ticket sales worldwide!

In the movie *Interview with the Vampire*, Brad Pitt played a vampire named Louis de Pointe du Lac. He was a young, rich man from New Orleans before being turned into a vampire.

STEP 1

Draw the head, and begin to draw the body.

STEP 2

Draw round shapes. These will help you draw the arms.

STEP 3

Join the round shapes to form arms. Add the hands.

STEP 4

Draw the hairline and the outline of the clothes. Draw the jacket and sleeve. Draw the stick.

STEP 5

Add the eyes, eyebrows, nose, and mouth. Draw the hair. Add the collar and other details to the clothes. Erase the guides.

STEP 6

Add the final details to the face and the clothes. Finish your drawing with color.

Grandpa Dracula

In 1964, a black and white television series called *The Munsters* showed the everyday life of a family of funny monsters. The father, Herman, looked like Frankenstein's monster. The mother, Lily, was a vampire, and the son, Eddie, was a werewolf. The grandfather, called Grandpa, was Sam Dracula, Count of Transylvania.

Grandpa was a funny and lovable character. As bats do, he slept hanging upside down. He could also **transform** himself into a wolf or a bat, just as Bram Stocker's Dracula did.

In 2012, *Mockingbird Lane*, a new television show based on *The Munsters*, showed Grandpa as a much scarier vampire than the first.

STEP 1
Draw an oval for the head. Add a shape for the outline of the body.

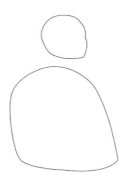

STEP 4
Draw the outline of the hair. Draw the collar and the front of the jacket.

STEP 2
Draw circles and ovals around the body.

STEP 5
Draw the eyes, nose, and mouth. Add detail to the clothing. Erase extra lines.

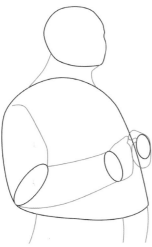

STEP 6
Add more details to to face and clothes. Color your drawing.

STEP 3
Join the circles and ovals to form the arms and hands. Draw the outline of the pants.

Eternal Life

Our image of vampires has changed throughout the years. One trait that has remained the same, however, is that vampires are immortal. They are said to be undead, existing in a strange state between life and death.

Being undead, vampires do not normally die. There are a few ways a vampire can be destroyed, though. One way a vampire may be destroyed is if it is exposed to sunlight. Another way to destroy a vampire is to drive a stake through its heart. In some stories, fire can also kill a vampire, as can cutting off its head.

STEP 1

Draw an egg shape for the head. Draw the body as shown.

STEP 2

Add shapes to serve as a guide for the arm.

STEP 3
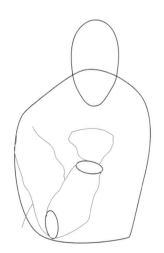

Join the guide shapes and draw the arm and hand.

STEP 4

Draw the outline of the hair. Add the detail to the front of the shirt. Draw the fingers.

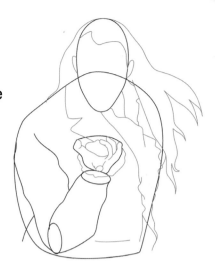

STEP 5

Add the eyes, nose, mouth, and ears. Add more detail to the clothes. Erase extra lines.

STEP 6

Give Dracula sharp fangs. Add the final details to his face and clothes. Color your drawing.

Some vampires are very different from the monsters of legend. They can be happy, silly, or friendly. Grandpa Munster was more funny than scary. And there is also Dracula from the 2012 animated movie *Hotel Transylvania*.

One of the friendliest and best loved vampires is *Sesame Street*'s Count von Count. He first appeared on the television show in 1972. The Count is known for counting everything sight. He is also known for his special laugh.

STEP 1

Draw the outline of the head and body.

STEP 2

Draw four circles to serve as guides for the arms.

STEP 3

Using the guide shapes, draw the arms and hands. Add the outline of the legs.

STEP 4

Draw the cape and jacket outline.

STEP 5

Add more detail to the cape. Draw the eyes, nose, and mouth. Erase the guides and any other extra lines.

STEP 6

Add finishing details to the face and cape. Color your drawing.

Monster Fun Facts

- Unlike other vampires, Polish vampires, known as Upier, and Russian vampires, called Upyr, sleep at night and wake up at noon.

- In many stories, vampires cannot enter a house unless they are invited. Often, however, they are able to use their charm to receive an invitation.

- Unlike witch hunts, vampire hunts went after the already dead. Hunting and slaying vampires was often simply digging up graves and destroying corpses.

- A rare disease called porphyria causes extreme sensitivity to sunlight, hairiness, strange behavior, and reddish brown coloring of the teeth. It is commonly called the vampire disease or the Dracula disease.

- The Bunnicula series is a popular series of books. It is about a vampire rabbit that feeds on the juice of vegetables.

Glossary

IMMORTALITY (im-mor-TAL-uh-tee) The quality of not being able to die.

LEGEND (LEH-jend) A story, passed down through the years, that cannot be proved.

GENERATIONS (jeh-nuh-RAY-shunz) A group of people who are born in the same period.

MYTHICAL (MITH-ih-kul) Based on old stories; not real.

PREY (PRAY) An animal that is hunted by another animal for food.

SPECIES (SPEE-sheez) A single kind of living thing. All people are one species.

TRANSFORM (trans-FORM) Change in shape.

Read More

Cloonan, Becky, and Gary Reed. *Bram Stocker's Dracula: A Graphic Novel*. New York: Puffin, 2006.

Ganeri, Anita. *Vampires and the Undead*. The Dark Side. New York: PowerKids Press, 2010.

Jungman, Ann. *Vlad the Drac*. London: Barn Owl Books, 2008.

Index

Websites

For Web resources related to the subject of this book, go to: **www.windmillbooks.com/weblinks** and select this book's title.